ARTMAKER™

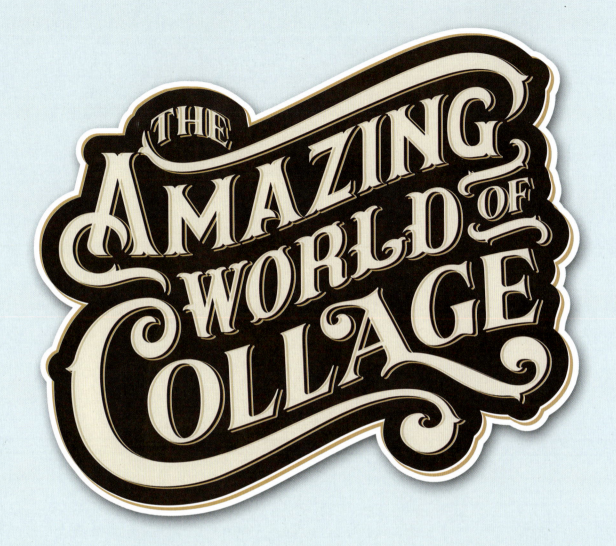

 Published by Hinkler Pty Ltd
45–55 Fairchild Street
Heatherton Victoria 3202 Australia
hinkler www.hinkler.com

Text and Design © Hinkler Pty Ltd 2025
Images © Hinkler Pty Ltd, Shutterstock.com or Adobe Firefly

All rights reserved. No part of this publication may be reproduced, stored in a retrieval system, or transmitted in any way or by any means, electronic, mechanical, photocopying, recording or otherwise, without the prior written permission of Hinkler Pty Ltd.

ISBN: 978 1 4889 6136 6

Printed and bound in Shenzhen, Guangdong, China

Contents

Welcome to The Amazing World of Collage 5

Creating Your Collage 6

Creative Sparks 8

Collage Pieces
    The Natural World 11
    Dreamscapes 35
    People 51
    Art and Culture 67
    Technology 85
    Domestic Life 95
    Cities of the World 101
    Miscellaneous 117
    Scenes 127

The Amazing World of Collage

Welcome to *The Amazing World of Collage*! Where you can turn random images into a creative masterpiece. A collage is a wonderfully fun artistic technique where you assemble different materials to create an artwork bigger than its parts. With a simple cut, arrange and paste of the images in this book you can create something new and totally captivating! But the art of collage isn't just about cutting and pasting. It's about storytelling and self-expression. From surreal and playful scenes, to complementary images woven together, the imaginative possibilities are endless!

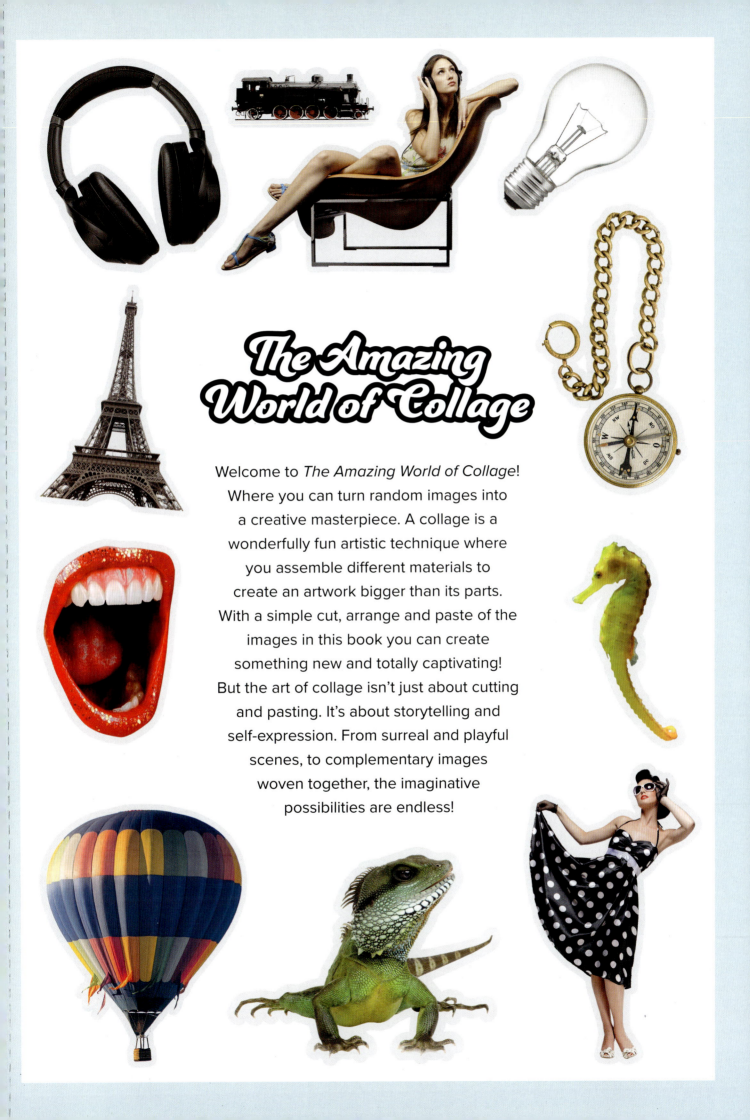

Creating Your Collage

YOU WILL NEED:
- Cutting board and craft knife (or scissors)
- Paper, posterboard, or traditional canvas
- Glue

OPTIONAL:
- Magazine clippings
- A pair of tweezers
- An acrylic sealer
- Adhesive putty
- Postcards
- Envelope
- Stickers
- Photos
- Tape
- Art supplies like markers, pencils, paintbrush and paints
- Fabrics and items of different textures, e.g. washi tape, ribbons, wrapping paper, string, chains, charms, sequins, buttons, beads, feathers, foil – be creative!

STEP ONE: Find a flat, well-lit, and clean workspace to gather all the materials you'll need to begin your collage. Place a protective surface down to prevent damage to your workspace, such as a cutting mat or newspaper.

STEP TWO: Choose a sturdy base for the foundation of your collage. You can opt for anything you like, but low GSM paper can be too thin and can damage easily. Try canvas, an upcycled wood panel, or cardboard. Consider how much space you'll need for your composition to determine the size and shape of your base.

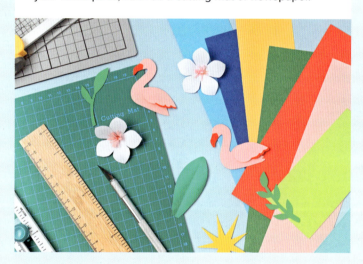

STEP THREE: Choose a background. Think of this as scouting the location for your story, as it will frame your entire piece. There are several backgrounds you can choose from in this book, or you can cut out an image from a magazine, use a blown-up photo, recycle old wrapping paper, or even add a little texture by using some aluminium foil.

STEP FOUR: Start flipping through this book (and your other materials) to select the images that align with your vision. Don't think during this process – just let your mind wander and pick out the images that resonate with you.

Handy Hint

Try to focus on the tactile nature of collaging. This has been proven to be therapeutic, allowing the mind to disengage from present troubles and instead focus on sensory exploration. This allows the artist to reconnect with their body and alleviate anxiety and stress, so it's important not to break the artistic spell by overthinking.

STEP FIVE: Create a collection of images for your collage. Using your craft knife and board, or a pair of scissors, roughly cut out your selected images without damaging others in the book. You can also rip whole pages out of magazines to save time. Cut out as many images as you want (any images that don't make the cut for this piece can always be used later).

STEP SIX: From your collection, start to cut out your images more carefully. Use a cutting knife and board for precise, clean lines and intricate borders, or opt for scissors if the image has a simple outline. Take your time and for safety, always cut away from your fingers!

STEP SEVEN: Start playing with your images against the canvas. With your chosen background as your base, experiment and see what compositions look good to you. If you find a position for an image that you love, use adhesive putty to secure it without permanently affixing it just yet. For precision or when working with smaller images, consider using tweezers.

STEP EIGHT: Once you've fallen in love with your masterpiece and are happy with the placement of all your materials, you can start permanently affixing. Simply use an appropriate glue or tape. Congratulations, you're now a collage artist! Put your artwork on display.

Handy Hint

- The story you are trying to tell – do you want it to be subtle? Clear? Satirical? Keep in mind the mood you want to create and see what arrangements work best to convey it.
- Have a point of view. Only you can create this work, so don't be afraid to take risks and make bold choices.
- You can add depth to the work by considering the background, middle ground, and foreground.
- You can overlap your images; this is an experimental art form, so don't be constrained by traditional constructs of what art should be.
- This is a playful process, so have fun!

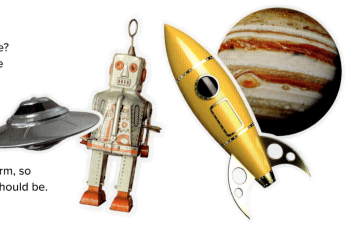

Creative Sparks

Need a little creative inspiration to create your first collage?
Here are some starting ideas.

NATURE-INSPIRED COLLAGE:

Create a vibrant collage by using different images from the natural world. Create depth and interest by layering up your images. Use nature-inspired tones like lush greens and earthy oranges. You could also combine your images with pressed flowers, seeds and dried-out leaves.

DREAMSCAPE:

Dream big with whimsical, futuristic, or fantastical collages. Focus on surreal imagery, mythological creatures, abstract shapes, and vibrant shades. Release the creative potential of your subconscious by using a wide variety of juxtaposing images. Challenge reality and let your imagination run wild.

MEMORY COLLAGE:

Take a trip down memory lane by creating collages that celebrate the people, places, and experiences that have shaped your life. You can use representative elements from this book in combination with your own photographs and mementoes to create personal and emotion-led narratives.

MIXED-MEDIA COLLAGE:

Mix things up by incorporating a variety of mixed-media techniques into one artwork, such as painting, drawing, and printmaking. Use art and culture as your subject to make a bold social or artistic statement. This will blur the lines between artistic forms and continue the evolution of collaging.

WRITE A MEMOIR:

Tell your unique story through a collage interspersed with writing and illustrations. Explore your rich inner world as you document your thoughts, feelings, and experiences through a technique that has proven psychological benefits. You could pick one important event or memory in your life or tell the story of someone who inspires you.

TRAVEL JOURNAL:

Document your travel journeys through a journal filled with collages and lists of your fave hot spots, restaurants, hotels, and historic sights. Fill it with the highlights of your trips around the globe. You could also create collage postcards while on your travels, by layering up images and mementoes from your trip to post home.

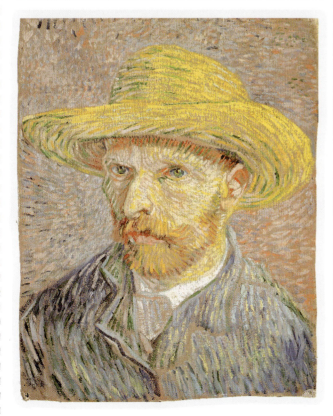

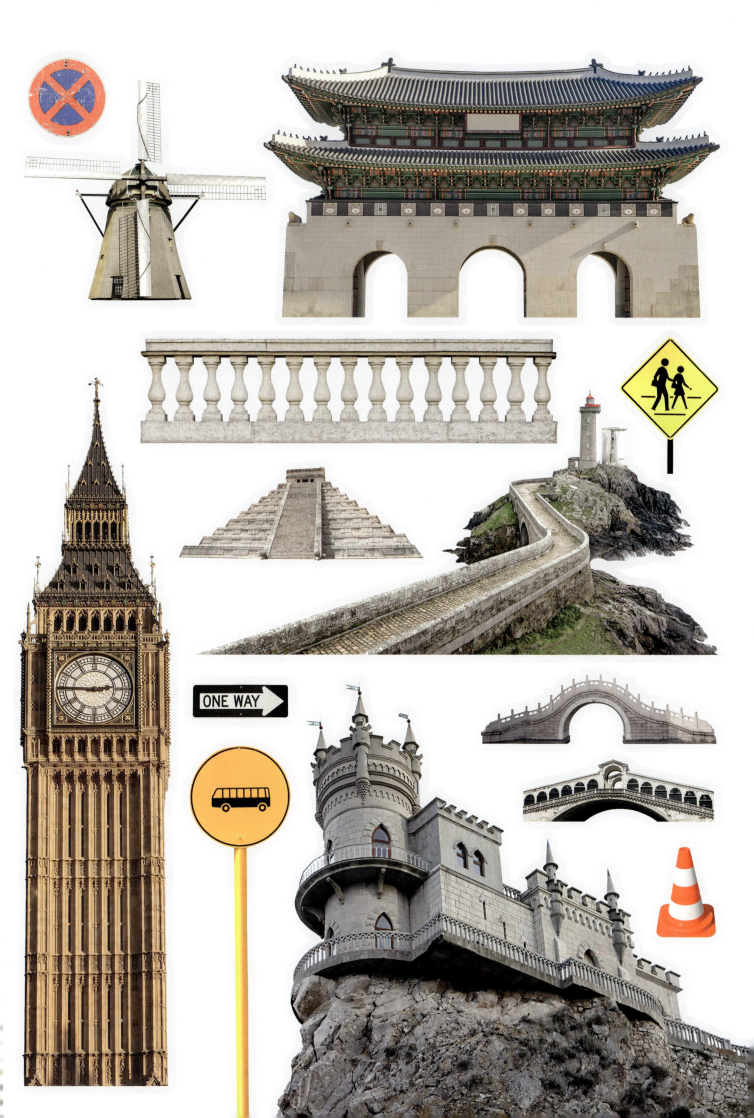

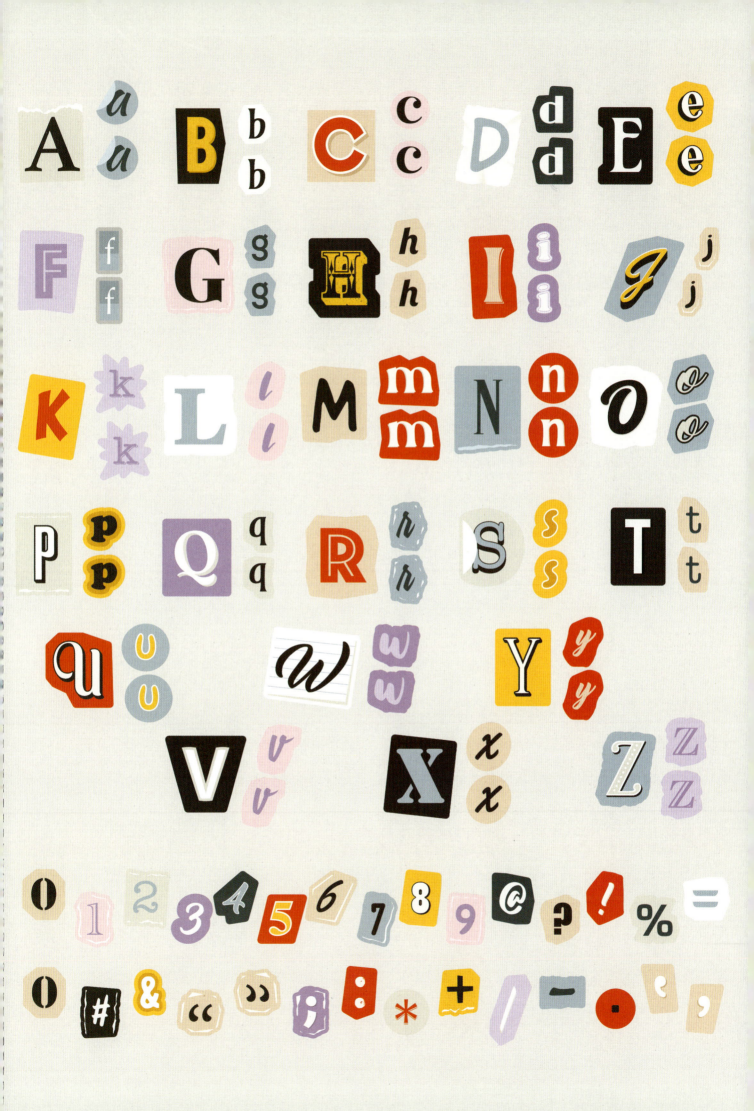

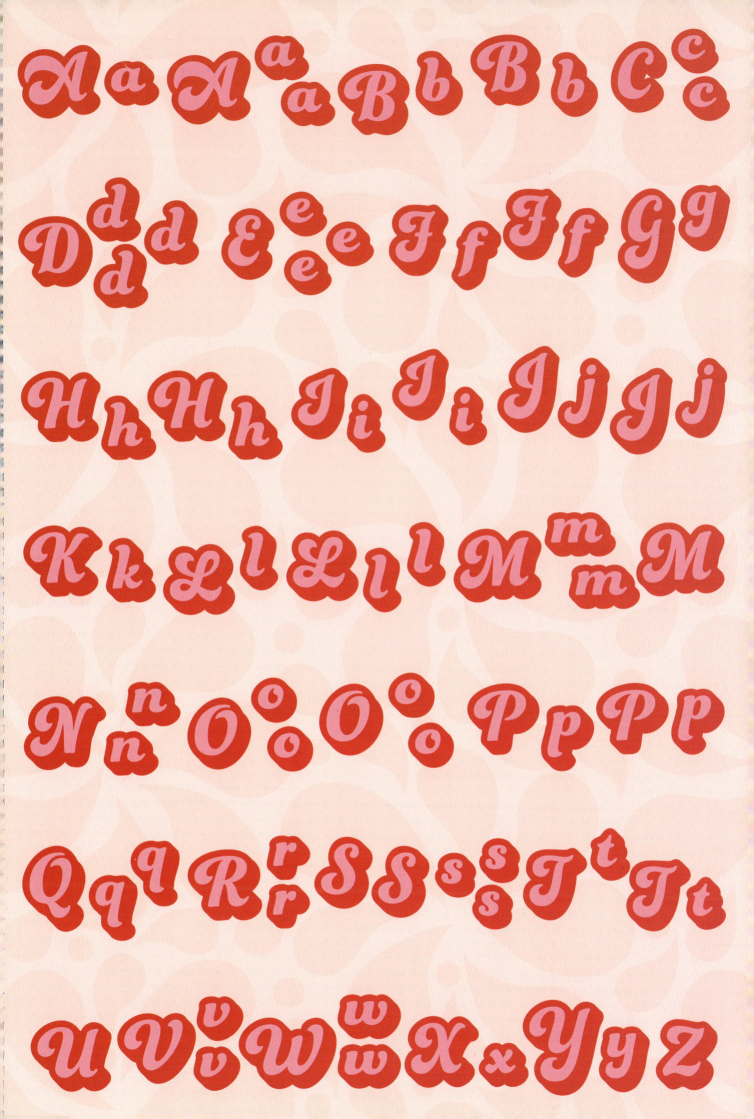